Let's Celebrate Latino Holidays

HISPANIC HERITAGE MONTH

Sadie Silva

Enslow PUBLISHING

Please visit our website, www.enslow.com. For a free color catalog of all our high-quality books, call toll free 1-800-398-2504 or fax 1-877-980-4454.

Library of Congress Cataloging-in-Publication Data
Names: Silva, Sadie, author.
Title: Hispanic Heritage Month / Sadie Silva.
Description: New York : Enslow Publishing, [2023] | Series: Let's Celebrate Latino Holidays | Includes bibliographical references and index.
Identifiers: LCCN 2021037520 (print) | LCCN 2021037521 (ebook) | ISBN 9781978527287 (library binding) |
ISBN 9781978527263 (paperback) | ISBN 9781978527270 (set) | ISBN 9781978527294 (ebook)
Subjects: LCSH: Hispanic Heritage Month--Juvenile literature. | Hispanic Americans--Juvenile literature.
Classification: LCC E184.S75 S53 2023 (print) | LCC E184.S75 (ebook) | DDC 973/.0468--dc23/eng/20211018
LC record available at https://lccn.loc.gov/2021037520
LC ebook record available at https://lccn.loc.gov/2021037521

First Edition

Portions of this work were originally authored by Marisa Orgullo and published as *Celebrating Hispanic Heritage Month!*. All new material this edition authored by Sadie Silva.

Published in 2023 by
Enslow Publishing
29 E. 21st Street
New York, NY 10010

Designer: Katelyn Reynolds
Interior Layout: Rachel Rising
Editor: Caitie McAneney

Photo credits: Photo credits: Cover, angelbandala/Shutterstock.com; Cover, pp. 1-4, 6, 8, 10, 12, 14, 16, 18, 20, 22-24 (background) Cienpies Design/Shutterstock.com; Cover, pp. 1, 3, 23, 24 (text box) scoutori/Shutterstock.com; Cover, pp. 1, 3, 23, 24 (text) Cienpies Design/Shutterstock.com; p. 5 ESB Professional/Shutterstock.com; p. 7 Ryan Rahman/Shutterstock.com; p. 9 Andy Dean Photography/Shutterstock.com; p. 11 Pixel-Shot/Shutterstock.com; p. 13 https://en.wikipedia.org/wiki/File:Sonia_Sotomayor_in_SCOTUS_robe.jpg; p. 15 BAKOUNINE/Shutterstock.com; p. 17 Tutti Frutti/Shutterstock.com; p. 19 Sundry Photography/Shutterstock.com; p. 21 Iakov Filimonov/Shutterstock.com; p. 22 Jemastock/Shutterstock.com.

Printed in the United States of America

Some of the images in this book illustrate individuals who are models. The depictions do not imply actual situations or events.

CPSIA compliance information: Batch #CSENS23: For further information contact Enslow Publishing, New York, New York, at 1-800-398-2504.

CONTENTS

Words in the glossary appear in **bold** type the first time they are used in the text.

Celebrating Culture

The United States is home to many different **cultures**. Each culture has special music, food, history, and **traditions** to **celebrate**. Americans celebrate **Hispanic Heritage** Month each year. It's a time to honor special traditions of Latin America. It connects Hispanic people to their home countries.

Many Hispanic families living in the United States still speak Spanish at home.

People celebrate Hispanic Heritage Month from September 15 to October 15 in the United States. Autumn is a time when several Latin American countries celebrate their **independence** from Spain. Some of these nations are Chile, Costa Rica, El Salvador, Guatemala, Honduras, Mexico, and Nicaragua.

In 1988, the U.S. government made this month a time for the country to honor all Hispanic Americans.

Hispanic Families

People came to the United States from Latin America for many reasons. Many Hispanic people live in places that were once part of Mexico. Others came from Central America, South America, or the Caribbean. They wanted to find safety, freedom, or jobs. Many Hispanic families call the United States home!

Hispanic families came from many different places for many different reasons.

More Hispanic families come to the United States each year. About 18 percent of people in the United States are Hispanic. Many Hispanic people live in the Southwest and in large midwestern and northeastern cities. They own businesses, such as restaurants and hotels. They work as chefs, doctors, reporters, and more.

Hispanic people are an important part of communities across the United States.

Famous Hispanic People

Some Hispanic people are famous for their work in art, sports, and government. From the 1950s to the 1980s, a Mexican American named Cesar Chavez helped gain rights for farm workers. Sonia Sotomayor was the first Hispanic U.S. Supreme Court Justice.

Sonia Sotomayor's family is from Puerto Rico.

Famous Hispanic people in sports include baseball player Alex Rodriguez and football player Tony Romo. Romo was one of the first Hispanic people to lead an NFL football team. Famous Hispanic people in music include Jennifer Lopez and Selena Gomez.

Selena Gomez is an actress and pop star with Mexican and Italian heritage.

Hispanic Americans have shared their **talents** and traditions in the arts. Hispanic artists paint, draw, and take pictures. Latin American music, such as salsa, is popular around the world. Latin American dances include the tango, salsa, and cha-cha.

The tango comes from Argentina.

Remember and Celebrate

European **explorer** Christopher Columbus arrived in the Americas in 1492. In the years that followed, Europeans killed many native people and wiped out many cultures. In October, many Americans celebrate Columbus Day. But many Hispanic people celebrate *Día de la Raza* (DEE-ah DAY LAH RAH-sah), or Day of the Race instead.

Many Hispanic people remember and celebrate their native cultures on *Día de la Raza*. They also remember and celebrate their loved ones who died on *Día de los Muertos*, or Day of the Dead.

Do you want to learn more about Hispanic culture? You can visit a **museum** to see Hispanic art, listen to music, learn a dance, or watch a movie. You could even learn some of the Spanish language! There are many fun ways to learn about Hispanic culture all year long.

Take a Hispanic dance class to learn something new!

The United States has many Hispanic Americans. They make up our communities. They are part of our history. Their traditions make our country richer. Celebrating Hispanic culture isn't just something to do for Hispanic Heritage Month.

You can do it all year round!

GLOSSARY

celebrate To honor with special activities.
culture The beliefs and ways of life of a group of people.
explorer Someone who travels to a new place to find information about that place.
heritage Something that comes from past members of a family or group.
Hispanic Someone who is from a Spanish-speaking country or whose family is from a Spanish-speaking country.
independence Freeedom from someone or something.
museum A building in which things of interest are displayed.
talent An ability to do something well.
tradition Something that has been done for a long time.

FOR MORE INFORMATION

Books

Reynoso, Naibe. *Be Bold! Be Brave! 11 Latinas Who Made U.S. History*. Los Angeles, CA: Con Todo Press, 2020.

Vourvoulias, Sabrina. *Nuestra América: 30 Inspiring Latinas/Latinos Who Have Shaped the United States*. Philadelphia, PA: Running Press Kids, 2020.

Websites

Hispanic Heritage Month
easyscienceforkids.com/hispanic-heritage-month/
Learn more about Hispanic Heritage Month and other holidays!

Hispanic Heritage Month
ny.pbslearningmedia.org/resource/4e982b0c-8c5f-4ebf-8add-ca692a1cc099/hispanic-heritage-month-all-about-the-holidays/
Watch a short video about Hispanic Heritage Month by PBS.

Publisher's note to educators and parents: Our editors have carefully reviewed these websites to ensure that they are suitable for students. Many websites change frequently, however, and we cannot guarantee that a site's future contents will continue to meet our high standards of quality and educational value. Be advised that students should be closely supervised whenever they access the internet.

INDEX